Cordially Invited

Have You Got What It Takes to Be an Event Planner?

by Lisa Thompson

Compass Point Books ✦ Minneapolis, Minnesota

First American edition published in 2008 by
Compass Point Books
3109 West 50th Street, #115
Minneapolis, MN 55410

Editor: Julie Gassman
Designer: Ashlee Schultz
Creative Director: Keith Griffin
Editorial Director: Nick Healy
Managing Editor: Catherine Neitge
Content Adviser: Irene E. Leiferman, Event Coordinator,
            Country Inn & Suites, Mankato, Minnesota

Editor's note: To best explain careers to readers, the author has
created composite characters based on extensive interviews and research.

This book was manufactured with paper containing
at least 10 percent post-consumer waste.
Printed in the United States of America.

Library of Congress Cataloging-in-Publication Data
Thompson, Lisa, 1969–
    Cordially invited: have you got what it takes to be
an event planner? / by Lisa Thompson.
        p. cm. — (On the job)
Includes index.
    ISBN 978-0-7565-3618-3 (library binding)
    1. Special events—Planning—Vocational guidance—Juvenile literature.
I. Title. II. Series.
GT3405.T46 2008
    394.2—dc22   2007035551

Image Credits: Istockphoto/nikada33, cover (left); Jupiter Images, cover (right).
All other images are from one of the following royalty-free sources: Big Stock
Photo, Dreamstime, Istock, Photo Objects, Photos.com, and Shutterstock. Every
effort has been made to contact copyright holders of any material reproduced in
this book. Any omission will be rectified in subsequent printings if notice is given
to the publishers.

Visit Compass Point Books on the Internet at *www.compasspointbooks.com*
or e-mail your request to *custserv@compasspointbooks.com*

Table of Contents

You're All Invited!

My office is buzzing with preparations. I am the event planner for an organization called the Wishing Tree Foundation, a charity that grants wishes to children in need.

My team and I organize all kinds of fundraising events, large and small, throughout the year. They include races, festivals, guest-speaker lunches, and film nights. The biggest and most exciting event to organize is our annual children's party. It is a chance for all the children who have been granted wishes in the past year to get together and celebrate life.

It is also an important event to attract media attention. When people see us on the news, we attract new donors and increase awareness of our work. This helps us gain sponsorship for the organization and organize future events.

It is my job as the event planner to make our events as successful as possible. As you are about to see, there's a lot more to planning an event than just picking a venue and sending out the invitations!

Before we get too far into the details for this year's event, I want to review what worked at last year's party. I filed a few notes away.

- Having something for the kids to do right when they arrive was important. It helped everyone become more comfortable.

- The entertainment needs to be age-appropriate. The guests liked the storyteller, but they loved the magician. I think it was better suited for their age group.

- The kids loved eating fun food, such as snakelike sandwiches, butterfly-shaped pasta, and dirt cake with gummy worms. More Please Catering came up with these great ideas, delivered on time, and was easy to work with.

PUN FUN Event planners who arrive late to parties will find they were beaten to the punch.

How I Became an Event Planner

Being an event planner requires a wide and varied set of skills. Like many event planners, I started out in another career. Because I loved the idea of traveling, I majored in tourism in college. Other planners get their start in business, marketing, or hospitality. After graduating, I got a job planning group tours of Europe. After a few years, I realized what I loved most about my job was seeing to the details. I've always enjoyed entertaining friends, so I thought event planning would be perfect for me. I was able to bring many of my previous job skills to the job of being an event planner.

Planners must be creative and organized, with excellent communication skills and the confidence to get the job done. They must come up with ideas to make events successful and be able to solve problems quickly. Planners must also delegate easily. They know how to give the responsibility for tasks to other members of their team. They also need to follow up quotes and requests.

Big or small?

The amount and complexity of an event planner's work can vary greatly—from big, internationally organized sports spectaculars (think the Olympic Games) to small, family parties. However, the goal is always the same: a meaningful, memorable, and successful event.

You could be planning something this big —

—or this small.

Whatever the size of the event, SUCCESS is the goal!

Be our planner

I am an in-house planner. In-house event planners work for a single company and may need to juggle many events at once. In the course of a year, an in-house planner can organize meetings, conferences, award presentations, corporate-sponsored events, product launches, marketing events, and annual galas.

Request the Pleasure of Your Compa...
Attire: Black tie – National Dress

What you need to be a good event planner:

✓ good organizational skills
✓ attention to detail
✓ strong interpersonal skills
✓ ability to delegate work and supervise others
✓ willingness to work irregular hours, weekends, and public holidays
✓ good communication skills
✓ professional grooming and presentation
✓ negotiation skills
✓ ability to work under pressure

Types of Events

Every event is unique, but you can place nearly every event into one of these four main types: leisure, personal, one-of-a-kind, and cultural. I love working on every one of these types of events. They each give me a unique opportunity to be creative.

Leisure: Any kind of sports or recreation event; for example, the Tour de France, golf tournaments, or charity races.

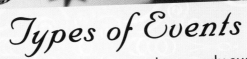

Tour de France

Personal: Weddings, birthdays, or anniversaries

One-of-a-kind: The Barham Street neighborhood barbecue, Garry and Ben's backyard snail race, or Emily and Sarah's fashion show

Emily and Sarah's fashion show

Snail race

Cultural: Ceremonial, sacred, heritage, or arts based, such as festivals, carnivals, or powwows

9

What Makes a Successful Event?

No matter what type of event it is, some things are always needed to make it a success.

Stand out from the crowd!

A good atmosphere is essential!

✓ **Uniqueness**
Even if an event takes place many times, like the Olympic Games, it's unique because of the different location, organizers, and audience. Creating a unique event makes the event surprising, memorable, and successful. It is a key part of the job of an event planner.

✓ **Ambience**
This is the atmosphere of the event. At a birthday party, where everyone knows each other, good company may be enough to create great ambience. For other events, the kinds of food, music, entertainment, decorations, and even when and where the event is held all help create the event's atmosphere.

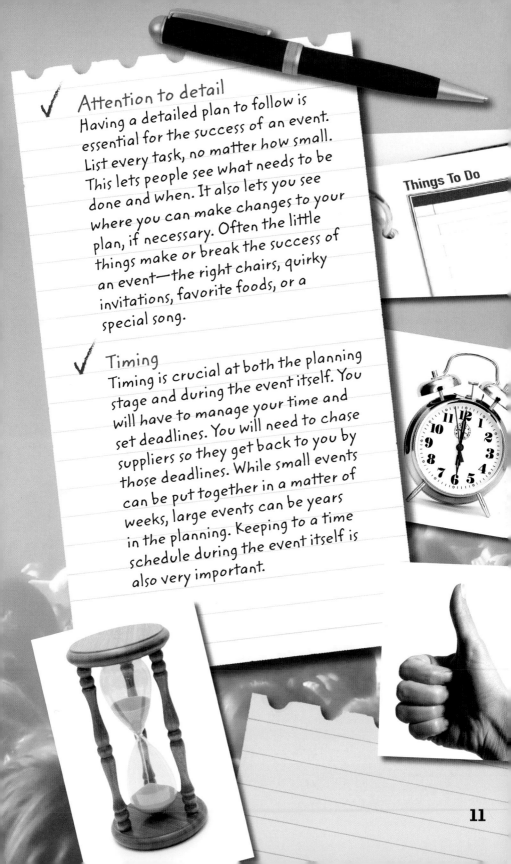

Attention to detail

Having a detailed plan to follow is essential for the success of an event. List every task, no matter how small. This lets people see what needs to be done and when. It also lets you see where you can make changes to your plan, if necessary. Often the little things make or break the success of an event—the right chairs, quirky invitations, favorite foods, or a special song.

Timing

Timing is crucial at both the planning stage and during the event itself. You will have to manage your time and set deadlines. You will need to chase suppliers so they get back to you by those deadlines. While small events can be put together in a matter of weeks, large events can be years in the planning. Keeping to a time schedule during the event itself is also very important.

Things To Do

Industries That Use Event Planners

Event planners may work in-house, for specialized event planning companies, for event suppliers, or as volunteers.

All kinds of industries and professions require event planners, including:

advertising companies	marketing agencies
the arts	museums
automotive manufacturers	nightclubs
beauty/cosmetic industries	public relations firms
communication suppliers	publishing companies
education providers	restaurateurs
entertainment industry	retail outlets
fashion industry	sports teams
hotels	tourism operators
governments	wedding suppliers

The list is as endless as the types of events to be organized!

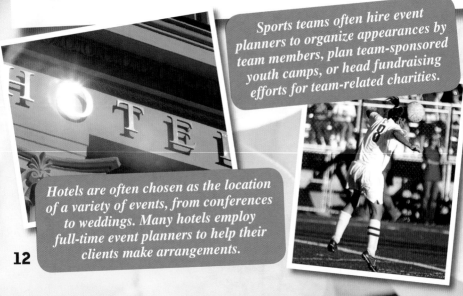

Sports teams often hire event planners to organize appearances by team members, plan team-sponsored youth camps, or head fundraising efforts for team-related charities.

Hotels are often chosen as the location of a variety of events, from conferences to weddings. Many hotels employ full-time event planners to help their clients make arrangements.

Automotive manufacturers roll out their latest designs at auto shows around the world. Event planners help iron out all the details for promoting the new cars.

Within the cosmetics industry, companies are always looking for new ways to get their products into the hands of beauty professionals and the customers themselves. An event planner helps create events where the makeup can shine.

Events are nothing new

Events have played an important part in society for thousands of years. Before we had TV, the Internet, or movies to entertain us, events helped to liven up the routine of daily life. And they still do today!

Family and religious events often celebrate life's milestones. They bring people together to recognize and witness important events— weddings, birthdays, baptisms, and so on.

Today many events still hold great traditional and cultural importance and involve ceremony and ritual. Others are personal and one of a kind. Whatever the event, most gatherings aim to enlighten, celebrate, entertain, or challenge those who attend.

PUN FUN When dressing up for a costume ball, disguise the limit.

From the Beginning

Some of the most popular events have interesting backgrounds. It's no wonder they are favorites of party planners everywhere.

Halloween

Halloween started as an ancient custom in the British Isles and northern France. There, the Celts marked the last night in October as the end of the year.

As the days grew colder and shorter with the coming of winter, people believed that ghosts, witches, and spirits haunted the nights. They built bonfires to chase away the evil spirits.

Over time, people began to go from door to door for food. In return, they would pray for lost souls. They believed that spirits would haunt people who didn't give anything.

Today millions of children around the world dress up in scary costumes. They take to the streets to trick or treat and collect sweets.

Hollowing out pumpkins has become part of Halloween.

The Olympic Games

The modern Olympic Games are loosely based on the games of the ancient Greeks. The first games, held in 776 B.C., had only one event—a 200-meter foot race known as the stade.

Later it included a pentathlon (the discus, long jump, javelin, a running race, and wrestling), a chariot race, a horse race, and the pankration (a violent form of wrestling).

The ancient Greek games lasted for five days as part of a religious festival to celebrate the most important Greek god, Zeus. Women had their own games for the goddess Hera. The games were organized by the temple priests of Olympia and had professional trainers, referees, and judges.

The ancient games continued, every four years, for about 1,200 years, until the Roman emperor Theodosius II closed them down in 393 A.D. The modern Olympic Games began again in Athens in 1896, followed by games in Paris in 1900.

Today the games are divided into summer and winter events, held two years apart. Together there are more than 400 Olympic events.

Birthday parties

In ancient times, only kings and queens celebrated their birthdays. No records were kept about other people.

The tradition of birthday parties began in Europe. People feared evil spirits were attracted to people on their birthdays. For protection, their friends and family would come over, bringing good wishes and presents to ward off the evil spirits.

Children's birthday parties began in Germany and were called *kinderfeste*. Today birthdays are the most common reason to have a party.

Events Celebrated Around the World

Every country has at least one unique event. Learning about the traditions and activities of other cultures helps me bring new ideas to my own events.

What: Moon Festival

Where: China

When: 15th day of the eighth month of the lunar calendar

The moon is full when Chinese people mark their Moon (or Mid-autumn) Festival. For them, the round shape means family reunion. It is a time for members of a family to get together. Sons and daughters return to their parents' houses for a reunion. Every Chinese holiday is accompanied by special food. For the Moon Festival, people eat moon cakes. This type of cookie is filled with sugar, fat, sesame, walnuts, yolks of preserved eggs, ham, or other foods.

What: La Tomatina

Where: Buñol, Spain

When: last Wednesday in August

La Tomatina started in 1944 as a simple tomato fight among a group of friends in the main town square. Now around 30,000 people descend on the town of Buñol (in the Valencia region of Spain) to throw more than 239,800 pounds of tomatoes at each other!

What: Hina Matsuri

Where: Japan

When: March 3

Hina Matsuri is the Doll Festival. It is a special day for girls to dress up, show off their best dolls (called *hina-ningyou*), and admire each other's collections. Families pray on this day for their daughters' health and happiness.

What: Kodomo-no-hi

Where: Japan

When: May 5

Kodomo-no-hi is Children's Day. It is mainly a celebration of the energy and ambition of boys. Boys hang big, brightly colored streamers in the shape of carp (called *koinobori*) out the window in the hope of becoming as strong and brave as the carp.

What: Day of the Dead

Where: Mexico

When: November 1

This day began when people believed that the spirits of people who had died would return to the world of the living. Now it is a day to remember loved ones who have died and to celebrate life. People go to the graves of their relatives and leave food and gifts. After feeding the dead, they return home and eat a big meal to celebrate life. The markets are filled with toy skeletons and skull-shaped candies.

Procession to remember the spirits and celebrate life

PUN FUN

When the skeleton went to a party, he had no body to dance with.

What's behind the word?

The word *carnival* comes from the Latin term *carne, vale*! which means "Meat, farewell!" This term refers to the traditional Christian custom of giving up meat and fasting during the 40 days of Lent. Carnival was originally the time just before Lent and was the last chance for 40 days to have fun and enjoy meat.

Edinburgh Festival
Scotland

Osenbach Snail Festival
France

Calgary Stampede
Canada

Naadam Festival
Mongolia

Hawaiian Iron Man
Hawaii

Running of the Bulls
Spain

Full Moon Party
Thailand

Birdsville Races
Australia

More events from around the world ... the possibilities are endless!

Getting Started

How I put together the Wishing Tree Foundation children's party

Step **1** **Planning**
Eleven months to go

Some events I can easily put together by myself, but for a large event like this one, I need a group of people. My first task is to put together a great team.

The team

- **Me** ... Because I am in charge of the project, my job is to make sure the event is a success and comes in on budget.

- **Leni** is my assistant. Her job is to keep track of the plans, chase the suppliers, and inform the volunteers.

- **Eric** is the light and sound expert. He'll organize the audio/lighting equipment and the entertainment.

- **David** has a marketing background. He will be handling the sponsors and promoting the event through the media.

Wishing Tree Foundation children's party

Step 1: Planning

- Build a team
- Decide on a theme
- Remember the five Ws

3.2

REC

Deciding on a theme

We meet with the Wishing Tree Foundation staff to brainstorm ideas and make a short list of possible venues and themes for the event. We keep in mind our budget and the type of event our guests have come to expect from our annual gala.

The five Ws

The five Ws of event planning will help us visualize the event and get the planning started.

What is the event?

Why are you doing it?

Who will be involved?

Where will it be held?

When will it take place?

What's behind a word?

The word *gala* comes from the Old French word *gale*, which means merrymaking. Therefore, a gala is a celebration.

Choosing guests

We look at the guest profiles of the people we want to invite and think of the kind of event that they would most like. Since we have hosted the party in various venues for the past five years, guests have come to expect a unique location as part of the event.

What is a guest profile?

A guest profile describes the people expected at an event. If you know their interests and tastes, you can put together an event they'll enjoy. A guest profile includes information such as age, gender, job, why the guest is invited, and any special areas of interest. This helps when planning menus, seating arrangements, entertainment, and the theme of the event.

Guest profiles
- Max Spencer
- Erica Allen

Guest profile: Max Spencer

Name: Max Spencer
Age: 9
Wish granted: To meet the local professional baseball team and to spend the day training with them
Pets: A fish named Fang and a dog named Dodger
Favorite food: Pizza

Name: Erica Allen
Age: 11
Wish granted: Funding to attend a special performing-arts school
Pets: A cat named Bolly
Favorite food: Chocolate

After much discussion, we agree on a short list of ideas:

- Pirate party on a boat in the harbor

- Beach party at Blue Cove

Pirate, zoo, or beach party?

- Wild Wishes party at the zoo

We then research the ideas, check the availability of the venues, and see how each idea fits into our budget and schedule.

23

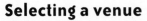

Selecting a venue

From the short list of venues, we decide that this year's gala will be a Wild Wishes party at the zoo. However, the Ostrich Cafe at the zoo, where events are normally held, is being renovated at the time we want to hold our party.

We must decide whether we want to change the venue or change the date.

After talking to people at the zoo, we decide to hold the event inside their special rain forest aviary. There is only one hitch. It is still being built! The zoo people promise us that it will be finished for our party.

The aviary is currently under construction.

This will be a very exciting venue. The space is filled with rain forest birds, animals, and plants, so our guests will feel as if they are really in the forest. We will be the first people to use the aviary for a function, so that makes it extra special. We just need to make sure it's finished in time!

A bonus is that the aviary is so large, we will be able to invite 100 children. That's 20 more than last year.

A date for the event is agreed on, and the venue is booked.

Now that I know the location and the seating capacity, I can start work on a more detailed budget and figure out how much there is to spend on food, entertainment, staff, and so on.

How much can we afford?

Organizing the Details

Now we have chosen the theme, location, and date of the event. It is time to put the event together.

I contact potential suppliers. I tell them our theme, venue, date, and the number of guests we expect to attend. We ask them to supply quotes for how much they think their goods and services will cost.

Don't forget to have fun!

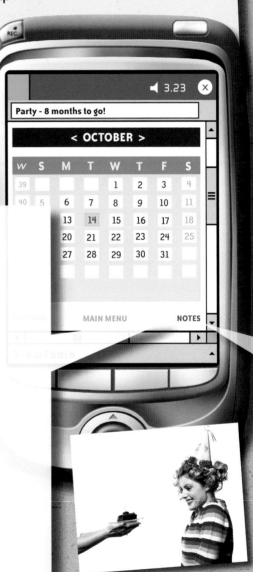

Party - 8 months to go!

< OCTOBER >

w	S	M	T	W	T	F	S
39				1	2	3	4
40	5	6	7	8	9	10	11
		13	14	15	16	17	18
		20	21	22	23	24	25
		27	28	29	30	31	

MAIN MENU   NOTES

What does a party need?

A list of supplies and services needed might include:

- ✓ furniture (tables, etc.)
- ✓ food
- ✓ music and entertainment
- ✓ serving staff
- ✓ flowers and decorations
- ✓ printed material (menus, name tags, etc.)
- ✓ stage, lighting, sets, and backdrops
- ✓ sound and communication equipment
- ✓ parking and security
- ✓ waste disposal and cleanup

Organizing an event involves dealing with many industries and suppliers. Who provides all these supplies and services?

Rental companies

Provide almost everything, from tents, tables, and chairs to plates, cutlery, glasses, and decorations

Caterers

Provide the food or chefs to cook on-site; also make recommendations for the menu

Security companies

Provide security staff to control crowds and keep everyone safe

Temp agencies

Provide the serving staff and grounds cleaners to clean up afterward

Florists

Create table centerpieces and may assist with interior design

Entertainment and stage companies

Provide music, MCs, DJs, comedians, etc., as well as staging and lighting; sometimes offered by separate companies

Printers/graphic designers

Print invitations, place cards, name tags, and menus

Leni collects the quotes and samples from suppliers. We visit some suppliers so we can test their stock on-site. The long list begins to shorten.

David talks to potential sponsors about supporting the event. Some companies offer their goods and services free to help the organization because it is such a good cause. David also talks to the media to promote the event and the zoo's new rain forest aviary.

We are all very pleased and excited when Eric manages to book a surprise guest as the master of ceremonies (MC) for the event. It is someone the children will be familiar with and excited to see. He is one of the young stars from a popular children's show— Tom Conway!

An MC is the leader of a party.

Party - 6 months to go!

< DECEMBER >

w	S	M	T	W	T	F	S
48		1	2	3	4	5	6
49	7	8	9	10	11	12	13
50	14	15	16	17	18	19	20
51	21	22	23	24	25	26	27
52	28	29	30	31			
1							

OPTIONS   MAIN MENU   NOTES

ViewTools

Being MC means Tom will act as the host of the event and be in charge of the games and entertainment during the party.

From the quotes Leni collected, I decide on the final list of suppliers that we will use.

4 MONTHS TO GO!

I discuss the look and content of the invitations with the graphic designer we selected. The invitations must contain complete information so the guests know exactly what the event is, why it is being held, where they are going, when they have to be there, and how to register their attendance.

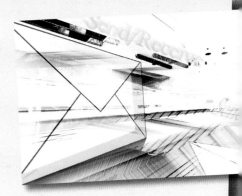

A week later, the designer sends a draft invitation for our approval. It is on green paper, in the shape of a large dragonfly. The wings have special folds to fit neatly inside an envelope. We check it carefully and mark up the changes we want. We send it back to the designer, who makes the changes and sends the final design to the printer.

An event planner tip on invitations

Not everyone can say yes to every invitation, so as a general rule, always expect two-thirds of all invitees to accept. Therefore, if you want 100 people at your event, you should send out about 150 invitations.

Something unique is a great way to get people's attention!

The invitations arrive eight weeks before the party, and my team sends them out right away. We give our guests two weeks to RSVP. Then we will know how many people are coming so we can make the food and seating arrangements.

Send all invites at the same time. That way you're less likely to forget someone!

What does RSVP mean?

RSVP stands for the French phrase *répondez, s'il vous plaît,* which means "please reply." The host is asking you to say whether you accept or decline the invitation. It is considered good manners to reply. It is also important for planning, since the organizer then knows how many people are coming.

More Please
CATERING

We have chosen More Please Catering to do the food. Belinda, the caterer from More Please, prepares samples of food that reflect the Wild Wishes theme. We need a variety of foods to cater to all tastes. Belinda has come up with some very yummy and clever ideas that incorporate the rain forest theme into all sorts of food in a fun and unusual way. There's bound to be something delicious for everyone!

Wild Wishes menu ideas

Rainbow sandwiches

Butterfly-shaped mini pizzas

Rain forest rolls

Yam pies

Mini frog quiches

Meatballs shaped like bugs and spiders

Barbecued chicken strips on sticks

Ladybug cupcakes

Gummy worms, jungle lollipops,
and chocolates

Bird- and bug-shaped candy and cookies

Bubbling beetle juice and butterfly nectar

More Please

C A T E R I N G

After negotiations to make the cost fit within our budget, we agree on the food for the party. I will get back to Belinda when final numbers are confirmed so she will know just the right amount of ingredients to buy and food and drink to prepare.

I immediately send the finalized list of food items to the designer so he can create the menu design, fitting in with our Wild Wishes theme.

2 MONTHS TO GO!

To our dismay, Tom, our MC, has to cancel. Luckily, he has arranged for one of his fellow cast members, Matt Tucker, to replace him. Eric has also booked the African drumming group Jungle Rumble, as well as a shadow puppet theater, to perform a piece from *The Jungle Book.*

Jungle Rumble—let's get the beats happening!

Shadow puppets

The team and I need to get creative to make a list of fun activities and games for the party. After a long afternoon of throwing around ideas, we choose our best:

- Bug race

- Design a bird mask

- Talk and tour with someone from the zoo

- Treasure hunt

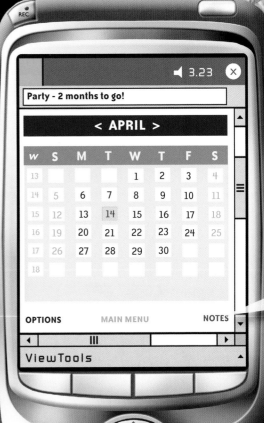

3.23

Party - 2 months to go!

< APRIL >

w	S	M	T	W	T	F	S
13			1	2	3	4	
14	5	6	7	8	9	10	11
15	12	13	14	15	16	17	18
16	19	20	21	22	23	24	25
17	26	27	28	29	30		
18							

OPTIONS   MAIN MENU   NOTES

ViewTools

The treasure hunt

The children at each table have their own treasure to find. The children follow the visual clues around the aviary, learning things about the rain forest as they go, until the last clue reveals the treasure!

X marks the spot! Or not ...

With two months to go, there are countless meetings. I consult with the zoo staff to organize the bug race, talk, and tour.

I meet with the temp agency to discuss waiter and staff numbers.

Then David and I meet with Eric to look at his draft list of lighting and entertainment requirements. David takes this information, along with a list of the dates the equipment is needed, to his sponsors. His job is to persuade them to provide what we need.

Does this look like a fast bug to you?

6 WEEKS TO GO!

Leni is constantly updating the list of those who have RSVP'd, and seats are filling up fast!

I get together with Eric to design a venue plan and finalize what is needed (and where) for the entertainment, lighting, and all the other necessary elements of the party.

This is just the rough draft!

Making a venue plan

A venue plan is a map that helps the staff set up the event space and see where everything and everyone needs to be, including:

- ✓ entertainment areas
- ✓ stage areas
- ✓ beverage and food areas
- ✓ seating arrangements
- ✓ audiovisual equipment locations
- ✓ power outlets
- ✓ restrooms
- ✓ emergency exits
- ✓ garbage areas

A venue plan helps you design the look and layout of an event. It also helps to identify planning challenges and possible solutions. For example:

- What kind of tables will best suit the number of guests—round, square, or rectangular?

- Are there enough power outlets?

- Can everyone see the stage?

- Do seating arrangements block emergency exits, or access to the kitchen or restrooms?

- Are the lighting levels right?

It takes a few drafts before we get the final venue plan right. We decide on 10 round tables with 10 children at each, and a stage in the center. This will allow the children to be close to the stage and all the action!

I consult a florist about centerpieces for the tables and discuss ideas to go with our Wild Wishes theme. He will get back to me with quotes.

TABLE DRAFT #36

10 kids per table

 PUN FUN The party planner wanted to use elaborate ceiling decorations, but they were over her head.

Since we are in the aviary for the gala, the restrooms are not within view of the tables. When hosting a party for children, it is especially important that they have easy access to restrooms. They will have to walk through another area of the zoo to find the restrooms, so I asked a few volunteers to be in charge of walking them there. (We don't want any lost guests!) The best part is they will get a look at the monkeys on the way!

We finalize numbers with Belinda, the caterer.

The florist's quotes come back. We negotiate a price we are both happy with, and I give him the green light to start.

To add excitement to the party, we decide to set up a welcome tent at the entrance of the zoo where our guests will meet. Inside the welcome tent, each child will receive a bag containing pieces to put together to make a mask. They will wear their masks in an animal procession to the rain forest aviary! They will also receive an animal stick. I ask Leni to arrange the making of the animal sticks.

We let Belinda know we have decided that each child will receive a goody bag of her jungle lollipops to take home, so she will need to make more.

Animal sticks

An animal stick is similar to a kite. Attached to each stick is a paper picture of an animal found in the upper level of the rain forest, such as toucans and monkeys. When the stick is gently moved in a circular motion, the animal flies around.

3.23

Party - 4 weeks to go!

< MAY >						
S	M	T	W	T	F	S
					1	2
	4	5	6	7	8	9
19		12	13	14	15	16
20	10		20	21	22	23
21	17	18	27	28	29	30
22	24	25	26			
23	31					

OPTIONS   MAIN MENU   NOTES

ViewTools

The rain forest aviary is officially finished and ready for us. We all breathe a sigh of relief, but now it is raining!

I have a meeting with the MC to run him through the event. The place cards arrive from the printer. I drop by the florist to see how the table centerpieces are looking. I am happy to say they look fantastic.

Leni is busy putting together the mask bags that the children will receive on arrival. She also picks up the animal sticks. The rest of the games still need to be organized.

Finally, five days before our event, the weather clears and the forecast is for sunshine for the rest of the week. We all keep our fingers crossed.

THURSDAY
12
JUNE
Final check at zoo today

I arrive at the zoo to oversee the setting up of tables and chairs. The lighting and power equipment is scattered everywhere because it is still being installed. The place is a mess.

Yikes! Boxes are already arriving in preparation for the party. Where can we put them? I know; how about the Ostrich Cafe kitchen? It hasn't been cleared for renovation yet—perfect!

Party supplies are arriving—we need storage space!

FRIDAY
13
JUNE
Meet volunteers today

Lights, volunteers, action!

The lighting and power equipment is all in place. I meet with the volunteers who will help with the procession, games, and activities. We run through the event and what we expect of them. They also help with setting up.

I take time out to give the volunteers a pep talk. I want them to get excited about tomorrow. They need to understand how important they are to the success of the event, and I want them to know that we appreciate all their hard work.

The tables are covered, but some tablecloths need to be returned and swapped: They are not what we ordered. The florist arrives with the centerpieces. Our volunteers put up the welcome tent, and the area is roped off.

Later that evening, Eric, Leni, and I finally finish putting together all the games and activities.

We're getting there!

Being an event planner is not only about organization. It is also about getting everyone involved excited about what they are doing. If you are energetic, motivated, and passionate, you will be much better able to inspire your team, suppliers, and volunteers to give 100 percent!

SATURDAY

14

JUNE

The BIG DAY!!

Give your performers time to prepare.

The big day arrives

Thankfully, the sun is shining and the weather is perfect. Some last-minute tweaking to the lighting and power equipment is done. The kitchen at the Ostrich Cafe has been cleared, and the caterer is busy delivering food.

The staff begins to get everything ready. They make sure everything is clean and set up for the party.

Jungle Rumble does a sound check, and the puppet theater performers set up their space.

The head staff members are briefed on the expectations for the event and are given a timetable of the activities.

The Event Timetable

Wild Wishes

10 A.M.	Food begins to arrive from the caterers
10:30 A.M.	Staff, the MC, the band, and the puppet theater performers arrive
11 A.M.	Delivery of mask bags and animal sticks
12 noon	Children start to arrive in the welcome tent; they quickly assemble their masks and volunteers gather to lend a hand
12:15 P.M.	Jungle drums sound; everyone puts on their masks and gathers their animal sticks; they are led to the rain forest aviary
12:25 P.M.	MC welcomes the guests; Jungle Rumble performs a welcome song; children find their tables with the help of the volunteers and look around the space
12:30 P.M.	Lunch begins
12:45 P.M.	The children eat while watching the puppet show
1:15 P.M.	Jungle Rumble performs and encourages the children to join in
1:45 P.M.	Refreshments
2 P.M.	Zoologist from the zoo brings in some rain forest animals and plants for the children to see up close and talks about them; each child gets a bug for the bug race
3:30 P.M.	Treasure hunt
4 P.M.	Goody bags are distributed as the children are picked up

At 12 noon, the welcome tent begins to fill with guests. Any shyness fades away as the children receive their animal sticks and put on their masks. They start to chat, mingle, and make friends. The atmosphere begins to build just as we had hoped.

By the time the jungle drums sound for the procession to the rain forest aviary, the gathering tent is filled with excited chatter. The children eagerly join in the animal procession through the zoo.

Everyone is eager to see inside the new aviary, and when they do, no one is disappointed by what they see. It's fantastic!

The kids loved the drumming! We couldn't stop them from dancing!

The children run around excitedly and explore the amazing space filled with birds, animals, and plants. Everything is alive! The food is gobbled up. The entertainment captures everybody's attention, and the games let everyone join in the fun. The event is a huge success!

Wrapping Up the Event

Step 3 — Finalizing

Even though the event is over, I still have lots of things to do:

1. Make sure all the equipment has been returned to the suppliers.

2. Make sure all the accounts have been paid.

3. Send out thank-you letters informing all the volunteers and sponsors of the success of the event. The new patrons who want to support us and the media coverage from the event will help us to make more dreams come true for children in need.

4. Organize follow-up stories with the media on the success of the event. I also want to promote the work that the Wishing Tree Foundation hopes to do in the future, and let people know about other events we have coming up.

Everything needs to be returned in good, clean condition.

FRAG.LE
HANDLE
WITH CARE

PAID

Already on the promotional trail for the next event

ON AIR

Once all these things are done, it's time to start planning next year's event. However, first I need to finalize the details for the fun run next week and the golf tournament next month— not to mention the fish-for-a-wish day coming up!

It's busy but rewarding work.

PUN FUN The party planner was always the first to arrive because he did not want to be second guest by anyone.

Thank You

Inform all those involved of the result. It's both polite and professional.

Lunch Thursday w/ Bill

Pick R...

Meeting 3pm TODAY!

To Become an Event Planner

- Finish your high school courses with the best grades you can get, especially in math and English.

- Go on to college. Courses in business administration and hospitality are useful. Or you can take specific event planning and management courses, which are becoming more popular. Planners need to supervise all parts of an event. Taking short courses in subjects like catering, photography, and floral arrangement will help you in the job.

- Volunteer as much as possible by assisting planners, working for charities, and offering to plan events for family and friends for practice. (Start with small, informal gatherings.) To become an event planner, you need work experience. This is one way to gain some.

- When you get a job, remember that being a successful event planner relies on having good working relationships with your suppliers and gaining a good reputation in the industry.

- Remain dedicated in order to be successful. You need to have knowledge in so many varied areas that you will always be learning and updating your skills. You may also need to work long hours and be available around the clock, especially just before a big event.

- Jobs in this industry are often not advertised, so networking is essential (through volunteering, associations, etc.). The good news is that event planning is a growing business.

BACKSTAGE

Finish here—what a view!

You'll get to see all the backstage action.

Start here.

Event planners can find work in a variety of fields:

- In-house for an event planning company
- In-house for a company, such as a hotel, that does regular event planning as part of its business
- Running your own event planning business
- Working for government departments or charities, organizing their fundraising or community events
- Offering a specialized service, such as wedding or conference planning
- Moving into related fields, including marketing and sales and food and beverage management

now hiring

must have a clue

Find Out More

In the Know

- Planners often work long hours in the period prior to and during a meeting or convention, and extensive travel may be required.
- Employment is expected to grow faster than average.
- Opportunities will be best for people with a bachelor's degree and some meeting planning experience.
- Meeting and convention planners held about 42,500 jobs in 2006.
- According to the U.S. Department of Labor, average annual earnings for meeting and convention planners (which includes event planners) in 2006 were $45,500. The lowest 10 percent earned less than $25,900, and the highest 10 percent earned more than $70,950.

Further Reading

Bonner, Lori. *Putting on a Party.* Salt Lake City: Gibbs Smith, 2004.

Greenberger, Robert. *Cool Careers Without College for People Who Love to Organize, Manage, and Plan.* New York: Rosen Publishing Group, 2007.

Jones, Jen. *Throwing Parties.* Mankato, Minn.: Capstone Press, 2008.

Pasternak, Ceel. *Cool Careers for Girls in Travel and Hospitality.* Manassas Park, Va.: Impact Publications, 2002.

On the Web

For more information on this topic, use FactHound.

1. Go to *www.facthound.com*
2. Type in this book ID: 0756536189
3. Click on the *Fetch It* button.

Glossary

ambience—general atmosphere or mood of a place or event

brainstorm—to think of solutions or ideas by considering every possibility

brief—to give instructions and information to complete a task

catering—providing food for a special occasion or event

delegate—to give another person responsibility for a task

draft—rough version of something; a work in progress

fundraising—raising money for a cause or project

gala—a festive celebration

hospitality industry—businesses that provide services that entertain guests

in-house—done within an organization and not by outsiders

invitees—people invited to a function or event

marketing—the promotion and sale of a service or product

master of ceremonies (MC)—person who directs activities at an event

negotiate—to discuss in order to reach an agreement about something

promotional—related to advertising through the media or by word of mouth

quotes—cost estimates from potential suppliers of services

RSVP—shortened form of the French phrase *répondez, s'il vous plaît*; means "please reply"

sponsorship—financial support of an event or project, usually in return for public acknowledgment

theme—main subject or topic; it determines the food, music, and decorations of a party

tourism—industry that encourages traveling for pleasure and provides related services

venue—the location where an event is held

Index

Look for More Books in This Series:

Art in Action: Have You Got What It Takes to Be an Animator?

Battling Blazes: Have You Got What It Takes to Be a Firefighter?

Creating Cuisine: Have You Got What It Takes to Be a Chef?

Focusing on Fitness: Have You Got What It Takes to Be a Personal Trainer?

Hard Hat Area: Have You Got What It Takes to Be a Contractor?

Pop the Hood: Have You Got What It Takes to Be an Auto Technician?

Sea Life Scientist: Have You Got What It Takes to Be a Marine Biologist?

Trendsetter: Have You Got What It Takes to Be a Fashion Designer?

Wild About Wildlife: Have You Got What It Takes to Be a Zookeeper?